BIBLE EASTER PUZZLES

by Richard Latta

illustrated by Joe Benjamin

Cover by Dan Grossmann

Shining Star Publications, Copyright ©1988
A Division of Good Apple, Inc.

ISBN No. 0-86653-427-X

Standardized Subject Code TA ac

Printing No. 9876543

Shining Star Publications
A Division of Good Apple, Inc.
Box 299
Carthage, IL 62321-0299

DEDICATION
To Mary, Tena, Sara, Tara
and Alyssa Latta

SS885

TABLE OF CONTENTS

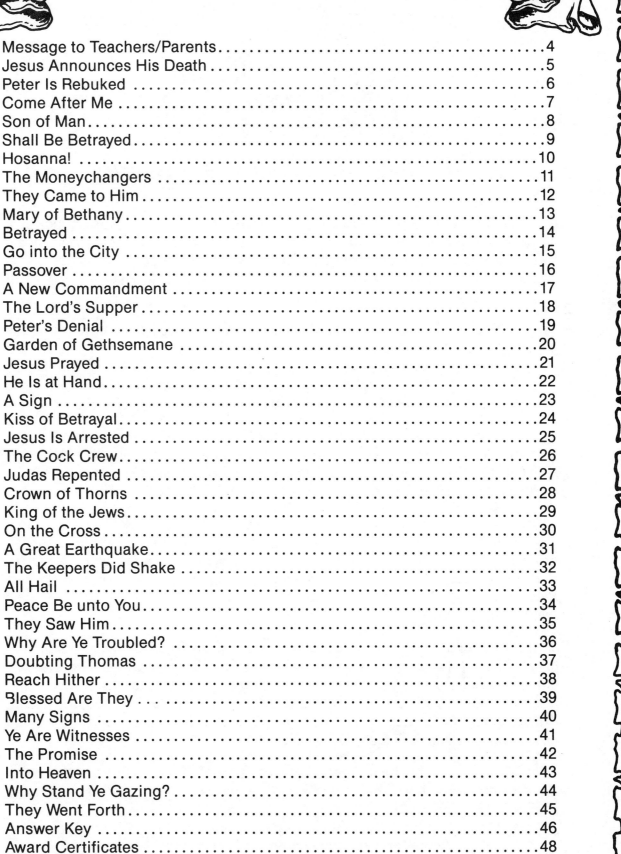

Shining Star Publications, Copyright © 1988, A division of Good Apple, Inc.

SS885

Message to Teachers/Parents

BIBLE EASTER PUZZLES was designed to lead your Bible students or your own children on a comprehensive journey from Jesus' prophecy in Galilee of His coming trial, death, and Resurrection to His Ascension from Bethany into heaven. The puzzles in this book will provide opportunities for children to learn all the important facts surrounding the Resurrection of Jesus.

"From that time forth began Jesus to shew unto his disciples, how that he must go unto Jerusalem, and suffer many things of the elders and chief priests and scribes, and be killed, and be raised again the third day." Beginning with Jesus' announcement to the Disciples, children will sequentially progress through specially designed puzzles, mazes and codes to learn the accounts of the first Easter.

"And as they were eating, Jesus took bread, and blessed it, and brake it, and gave it to the disciples, and said, 'Take, eat; this is my body.' " The Lord's Supper, the Garden of Gethsemane, Peter's denial, and Judas' betrayal, all unfold as children complete these Scripture-based activities.

"Now when the centurion, and they that were with him, watching Jesus, saw the earthquake, and those things that were done, they feared greatly, saying, Truly this was the Son of God." Children will learn the sad details of Jesus' Crucifixion, but they will also rejoice as they learn the facts of His glorious Resurrection! "He is not here: for he is risen, as he said, Come, see the place where the Lord lay."

Then Jesus appeared to His Disciples many times after His Resurrection and before His Ascension into heaven. Children will study about Doubting Thomas and the other events that occurred in the days between the Resurrection and the Ascension. "And there are also many other things which Jesus did, the which, if they should be written every one, I suppose that even the world itself could not contain the books that should be written."

SPECIAL NOTE: The King James Version of the Bible was used in preparing the activities in this book. Be sure to have one on hand when working the puzzles in BIBLE EASTER PUZZLES.

SS885

JESUS ANNOUNCES HIS DEATH

While in Galilee, Jesus told the Disciples of His coming trial, death, and Resurrection. To discover what the Bible says about this, you must put spaces between words and reverse the letters of some words. To check your work, read Matthew 16:21.

"M O R F / T H A T / E M I T / H T R O F B E G A N S U S E J T O W E H S

From   that   time _____

O T N U H I S S E L P I C S I D H O W T A H T E H T S U M G O

_____

U N T O M E L A S U R E J D N A R E F F U S M A N Y S G N I H T

_____

O F E H T E L D E R S A N D F E I H C S T S E I R P A N D

_____

S E B I R C S A N D E B D E L L I K

_____

D N A E B D E S I A R A G A I N

_____

E H T D R I H T Y A D."

_____

SS885

PETER IS REBUKED

The Disciples were puzzled when Jesus spoke of coming events. Peter was angry when Jesus told the Disciples about His coming death and Resurrection. To discover what Peter said to Jesus, you must decide what line in each letter found below doesn't belong. Rewrite the letters on the lines under each word to form words. To check your answer, read Matthew 16:22.

"ⵊⴰⴱⵏ   ⴰⴱⵊⴱⴱ   ⵊⵔⵇⴽ

<u>T H E N</u>   _____   _____

ⴰⵜⵏ,   ⴰⵏⴱ   ⴱⴰⴳⴰⵏ

_____   _____   _____

ⵊⵔ   ⴱⴻⴱⵏⴽⴱ   ⴰⵍⵏ,

____   _____   ____

ⵙⵊⴰⵢⵜⵏⴳ,   ⴱⴱ   ⵊⵜ

_____   ____   ___

ⴰⴰⴱ   ⴰⴱⵔⵏ   ⵜⴰⴻⴳ,

____   _____   _____

ⵏⵓⴱⴱ: ⵊⴰⵜⴱ   ⴱⴰⴰⵍⵍ

_____   _____   _____

ⵏⵔⵊ   ⴱⴱ   ⵡⵏⵜⴱ   ⵊⴰⴱⴱ."

____   ___   _____   _____

Use this secret code to write Matthew 16:23. See if your friend can read your message.

SS885

COME AFTER ME

When Peter rebuked Jesus, Jesus said to Peter, "Get thee behind me, Satan: thou art an offence unto me: for thou savourest not the things that be of God, but those that be of men." Then Jesus told his Disciples something very important. To discover what He said, use the number and letter code to decode Matthew 16:24.

"B3   _____   D4 _____   E1 _____   A5 _____
   Then

B1 _____   C2 _____   C4 _____   A2 _____

E5 _____   B5 _____   D1 _____   D3 _____

E3 _____   D5 _____   A4 _____   A3 _____

D2 _____   C3 _____   A1 _____

C5 _____   B4 _____   C1 _____

B2 _____   E2 _____

E4 _____ "

	1	2	3	4	5
A	take	any	deny	him	unto
B	his	and	Then	his	will
C	cross,	disciples,	and	If	up
D	come	himself,	after	said	let
E	Jesus	follow	me,	me.	man

Use this kind of code to write Matthew 16:25, 26, or 27.

SS885

SON OF MAN

Jesus said, "For whosoever will save his life shall lose it: and whosoever will lose his life for my sake shall find it." Then Jesus made a promise about the coming kingdom. To discover what this promise was, follow the path from GO to FINISH combining the consonants and vowels in each circle to form words. When you reach the end of the path, check your work by reading Matthew 16:28.

...ar Publications, Copyright © 1988, A division of Good Apple, Inc.

SS885

SHALL BE BETRAYED

Follow the circles from START to STOP. To correctly write Matthew 17:22, you must choose the correct words from the diamond touching each circle and write them in the circles.

Create your own circle maze and put the words from Matthew 17:23 in the diamonds touching the circles. Don't fill in the answers. See if a friend can solve your puzzle.

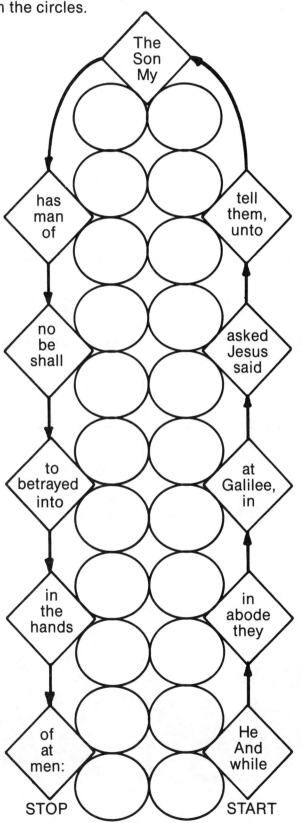

The
Son
My

has
man
of

tell
them,
unto

no
be
shall

asked
Jesus
said

to
betrayed
into

at
Galilee,
in

in
the
hands

in
abode
they

of
at
men:

He
And
while

STOP

START

SS885

⊰ HOSANNA! ⊱

While on the way to the Passover feast in Jerusalem, Jesus sent two Disciples to the next village to find a donkey and her colt. Find out what happened when Jesus rode the donkey slowly into Jersualem by dropping the words into the correct squares found below them. Some of the words have been filled in for you. Check your work by reading Matthew 21:9.

name David: And	of the cried,	saying, the is	that Hosanna he	went Hosanna that	cometh the before,	son and in	of that highest.
		multitudes					
followed,				to			
	Blessed						the
			Lord;		in	the	

Use this puzzle format to create a puzzle using the words found in Matthew 21:10 or 21:11.

SS885

THE MONEYCHANGERS

"And Jesus went into the temple of God, and cast out all them that sold and bought in the temple, and overthrew the tables of the moneychangers, and the seats of them that sold doves." Find out what Jesus said to the moneychangers by writing the letters found outside each circle, clockwise or counterclockwise, in each circle found below. Read Matthew 21:13 to check your answer.

SS885

THEY CAME TO HIM

To discover what happened after Jesus overturned the tables of the money-changers, use the code to decode Matthew 21:14.

A-1,   B-2,   C-3,   D-4,   E-5,   F-6,   G-7,   H-8,   I-9,   J-10,
K-11, L-12, M-13, N-14, O-15, P-16, Q-17, R-18, S-19, T-20,
U-21, V-22, W-23, X-24, Y-25, Z-26

"1 14 4   20 8 5   2 12 9 14 4   1 14 4
And   _____   _____   _____   _____

20 8 5   12 1 13 5   3 1 13 5   20 15
_____   _____   _____   _____

8 9 13   9 14   20 8 5   20 5 13 16 12 5;
_____   _____   _____   _____

1 14 4   8 5   8 5 1 12 5 4   20 8 5 13."
_____   _____   _____   _____

Use the number code to write
Matthew 2:15.

SS885

MARY OF BETHANY

While in Bethany in the house of Simon, a leper, something happened to Jesus. Can you find a path through the maze of words that tells what happened to Jesus? Check your answer by reading Matthew 26:7.

precious	very	alabaster	an
ointment	of	box	
	poured	it	having
and	on	his	
	him	a	woman
at	sat	head	
	unto	came	There START
meat	he	as	

SS885

BETRAYED

One of the twelve Disciples, Judas Iscariot, went to the chief priests and made an agreement to deliver Jesus to them. To find out more about Judas' covenant to betray Jesus, you will need to add the correct vowels to the consonants listed below. Check your work by reading Matthew 26:15, 16.

"nd	sd	nt	thm,	Wht
And	_said_	_____	_____	_____

wll	y	gv	m,	nd
_____	_____	_____	_____	_____

I	wll	dlvr	hm	nt
_I_	_____	_____	_____	_____

y?	nd	thy	cvnntd	wth
_____	_____	_____	_____	_____

hm	fr	thrty	pcs	f
_____	_____	_____	_____	_____

slvr.	nd	frm	tht	tm
_____	_____	_____	_____	_____

h	sght	pprtnty	t
_____	_____	_____	_____

btry	hm."
_____	_____

Shining Star Publications, Copyright © 1988, A division of Good Apple, Inc. SS885

GO INTO THE CITY

The first day of the feast of unleaven bread, the Disciples asked Jesus, "Where will we prepare and eat the Passover meal?" To discover what Jesus said to the Disciples, you will have to rewrite the Bible verse Matthew 26:18 found below. The letters of each word are in the correct order, but spaces have been placed between letters in the same word and some spaces between words have been left out. Check the Scriptures after you finish your work.

An   d/he/s   a   id/g   o

And   he   said

in   tot   he   cit   ytos

uch   a   ma   nan   dsa

yun   toh   imt   hem

a   sters   a   it   hmyt

i   me   i   sat   han

diw   ill   ke   ept   hep

as   sove   rat   th   yho

use   wit   hmydi   sci   ples.

SS885

PASSOVER

The Disciples did as Jesus told them and prepared the Passover. To discover what happened the evening of Passover, use the words in the blocks to complete the Bible verses Matthew 26:20, 21. Use the one letter and number of letters given for each word as clues.

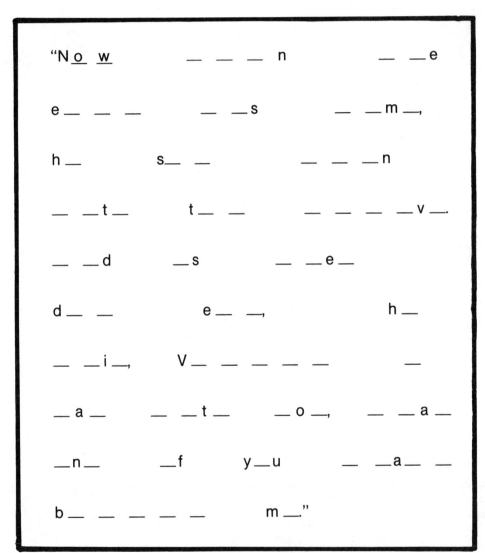

"N o w _ _ _ n _ _e

e_ _ _ _ _s _ _m _,

h _ s_ _ _ _ _n

_ _ t _ t_ _ _ _ _ _ _ _v _.

_ _ d _s _ _e _

d _ _ e _ _, h _

_ _ i _, V_ _ _ _ _

_ a _ _ _ t _ _ o _, _ _ a _

_ n _ _ f y _ u _ _ a _

b _ _ _ _ _ m _."

of
betray
l
did
the   as
eat,
me.   he
was
sat   one
when
that   say
with
Now   even
Verily   And   shall   unto   you,   down
you   they   said,   twelve.   he   come,   the

SS885

A NEW COMMANDMENT

Jesus told the Disciples, "Where I go, ye cannot come." And He gave them a new commandment. Read the commandment in John 13:34. Write it below.

"_____

_____

_____

_____

_____"

Next find each word of the new commandment hidden in the picture found below.

THE LORD'S SUPPER

To discover what Jesus said to His Disciples at the Last Supper, simply draw a line like you are lacing a shoe from one column of words to the next. After you have connected all the words with a line, write the words in the order they are found. Check your work by reading Matthew 26:26.

And	body.
my	as
they	is
this	were
eating,	eat;
Take,	Jesus
took	said,
and	bread,
and	disciples,
the	blessed
it,	to
it	and
brake	gave
and	it,

"And as they _____

_____

_____

_____

_____

_____

_____ "

Use this shoelace puzzle format to write Matthew 26:30. Give your puzzle to a friend to solve.

Find out more of Jesus' words at the Last Supper by completing this puzzle.

And	sins.
of	he
took	remission
the	the
cup,	for
many	and
gave	for
shed	thanks,
and	is
which	gave
it	testament,
new	to
them,	the
of	saying,
Drink	blood
my	ye
all	is
this	of
it;	For
"	

_____

_____

_____

_____

_____ "

SS885

PETER'S DENIAL

Jesus' prophecy concerning Peter's denial is told in Matthew 26:31-35. Peter said, "Though all *men* shall be offended because of thee, *yet* will I never be offended." To discover what Jesus answered Peter, place the words found below in the correct order by listing the words in numerical sequence.

deny 384	say 118	me 418
cock 280	him 80	I 101
thrice 4018	said 34	crow 308
Jesus 3	the 223	thee 133
Verily 99	unto 56	That 138
unto 121	night 187	this 145
shalt 350	thou 333	before 200

" _____ _____ _____ , _____ _____ _____

_____ _____ , _____ _____ _____ , _____ _____

_____ _____ , _____ _____ _____ _____ _____ . "

Create a puzzle with the same format using the Bible verse, Matthew 26:35.

SS885

GARDEN OF GETHSEMANE

Jesus and His Disciples went to a place called Gethsemane. Jesus said, "Sit ye here, while I go and pray yonder." He took Peter and two other Disciples with Him. What did Jesus say to the three Disciples? Read Matthew 26:38. Write the Bible verse below. Then place each word found in the verse in the puzzle. Use the number of letters in each word as clues to get you started.

"

_____

_____

_____

_____ "

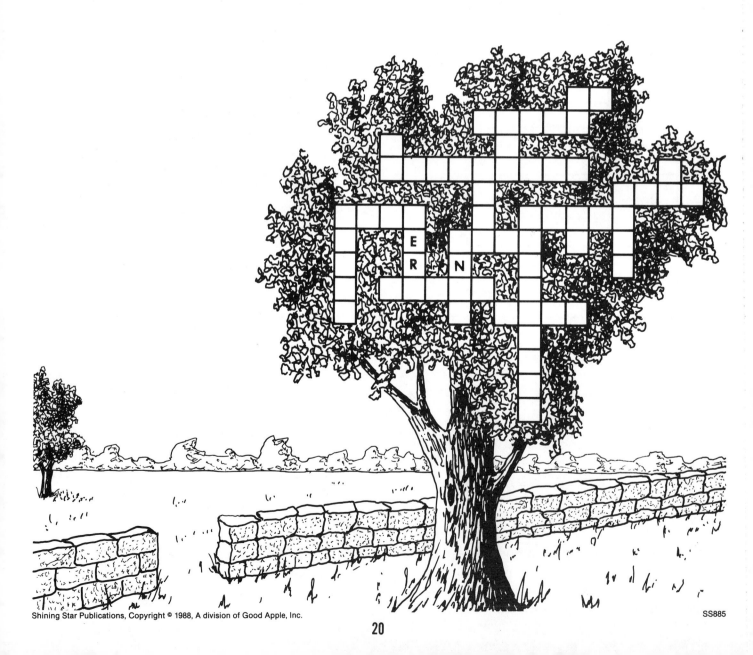

SS885

JESUS PRAYED

Jesus went a little farther into the Garden of Gethsemane and prayed, "O my Father, if it be possible, let this cup pass from me: nevertheless not as I will, but as thou *wilt*." Then Jesus found the Disciples sleeping. What did Jesus say to His sleeping Disciples and what did He pray afterwards? To discover the answers, write the letters in order as they are found on the bramble bush, putting spaces between words. Check your work by reading Matthew 26:41, 42.

"
_____

_____

_____

_____

_____
"
_____

HE IS AT HAND

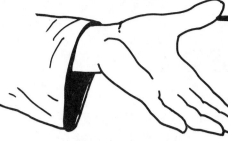

When Jesus returned a second time and found the Disciples still sleeping, He asked them an important question. To discover the question Jesus asked His Disciples and the startling news he brought, unscramble the words found below. Write the word on the line under each scrambled word. Check your answer by reading Matthew 26:45.

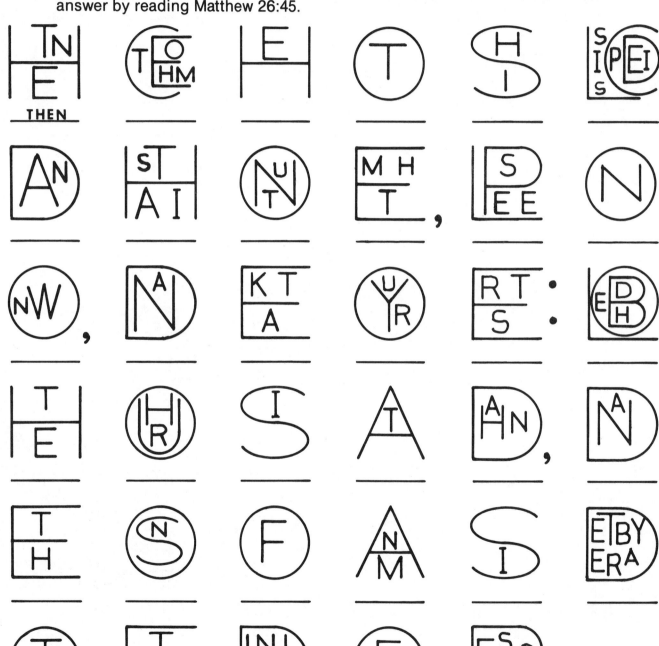

THEN

Create your own puzzle like this by scrambling the letters in Matthew 26:46.

SS885

A SIGN

While Jesus was telling His Disciples that His betrayer was near, Judas came with soldiers to arrest Jesus. Judas had promised the soldiers he would give them a sign to let them know which man was Jesus. To discover what the sign was, read Matthew 26:48. Write the Bible verse on the lines below. Then find and circle every word in the verse hidden in the letter maze. The words may read down, across or diagonally.

"
_____
_____
_____
_____
                                                        "
_____

n o w i s f i w
s h t a a a t w h
a o h b m s h o
y l a e e t a m
i d t t h s t s
n s x r x i s o
g x g a v e m e
h i m y a s k v
p t h e m i i e
o p e d x g s r
s h a l l n s x

KISS OF BETRAYAL

Judas' plan to betray Jesus was carefully executed. To discover what the Bible says about Judas' betrayal, add one line to each set of lines and form letters. Check your answers by reading Matthew 26:49.

Create your own puzzle like this one using the words found in Matthew 26:50.

SS885

JESUS IS ARRESTED

They arrested Jesus and led Him away to Caiaphas the high priest, where the scribes and the elders were assembled. Why did the chief priests, and elders, and all the council want Jesus arrested? Read Matthew 26:59, 60a to find out. Write the Bible verses below. Then find a path through the word maze that passes over each word of the Scriptures in order.

"_____

_____

_____

_____ "

GO ➜	Now	the	chief	priests	and	elders	false	witnesses	against
chief	the	chief	all	the	council,	and	many	false	Jesus,
priests,	and	elders,	and	council,	sought	council,	though	witnesses	to
and	false	witness	against	sought	false	sought	yea,	came,	yet
elders,	sought	against	witness	false	witness	false	none:	yea,	found
and	council	Jesus,	against	witness	against	Jesus,	found	none:	they
council,	sought	to	put	him	to	death;	But	found	none.
sought	false	witness	against	Jesus,	to	put	him	none:	END

THE COCK CREW

When Jesus was arrested, Peter followed Him to the high priest's palace. Later Peter was questioned about Jesus and he denied knowing Him. Then Peter denied knowing Jesus two more times before something happened to remind him of Jesus' prophecy. To discover what the Bible says about Peter's denial, write words for the picture clues found below. Check your work by reading Matthew 26:75.

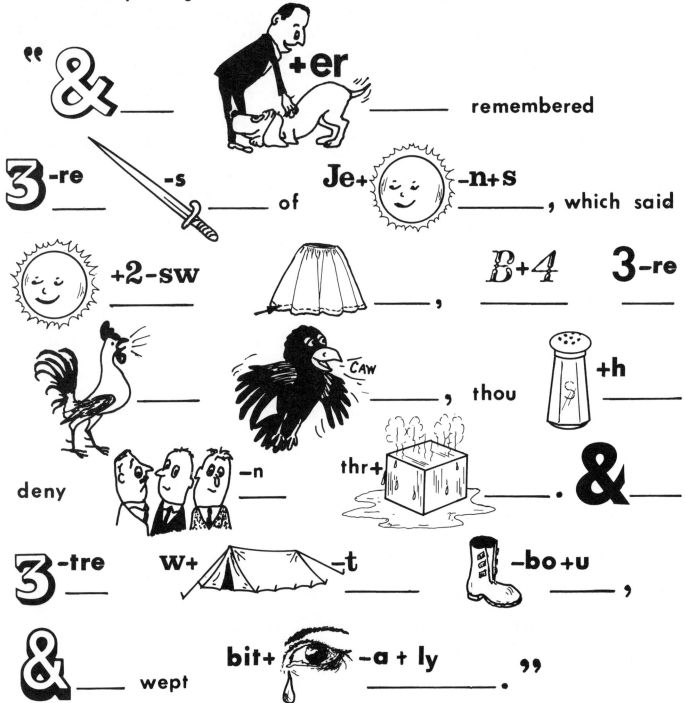

" & _____ +er _____ remembered

3-re _____ -s _____ of Je+ ☀ -n+s _____, which said

☀ +2-sw _____ (skirt) _____, B+4 3-re _____

(rooster) _____ (crow) CAW _____, thou $ +h _____

deny (men) -n _____ thr+ (ice) _____. & _____

3-tre _____ w+ (tent) -t _____ (boot) -bo+u _____,

& _____ wept bit+ 👁 -a+ly _____. "

SS885

JUDAS REPENTED

When Judas realized that Jesus was condemned to die, he was sorry that he had betrayed Jesus. He took the thirty pieces of silver back to the chief priests and elders. To discover what Judas did next, you must solve this puzzle. Begin with the first vertical row and go from top to bottom, recording each letter (found to the left of the dots) on the blanks below. Check your work by reading Matthew 27:5.

"<u>A</u> <u>n</u> _ _ _ _ _ _ _

_ _ _ _ _ _ _ _

_ _ _ _ _ . . _ _ _

_ _ _ _ _ _ _ _ _ _ _ _ ."

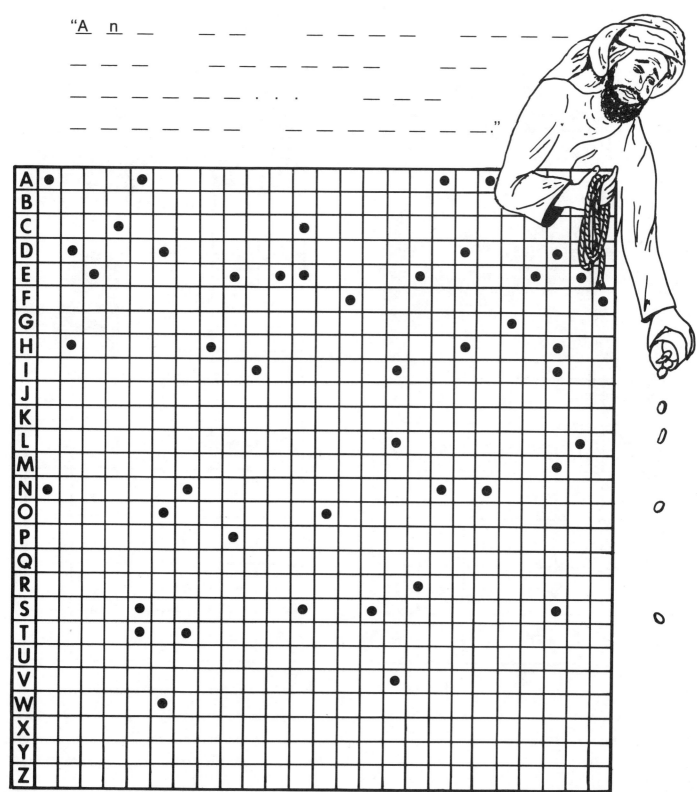

SS885

CROWN OF THORNS

The soldiers took Jesus into the common hall and gathered a whole band of soldiers around Him. The soldiers mistreated Jesus before they crucified Him. To find out more about this story, trace the decoder found below onto a piece of paper. Cut out the black squares. Place the cutouts over the group of letters with the word *top* at the top. Go from left to right, recording the letters visible through the holes. Next, turn the cutout a quarter turn clockwise and record the letters again. Continue turning and recording letters until you have solved the first puzzle. Then do the same thing with the second group of letters. Check your answers by reading Matthew 27:28, 29.

TOP

p	u	e	p	e	t
T	t	r	d	o	b
h	e	e	y	s	t
a	s	c	h	a	r
i	m	h	a	r	l
n	i	m	d	i	p

o	r	o	c	r	n
T	n	h	o	i	s
h	e	h	y	m	a
s	p	u	w	t	i
n	o	e	f	d	t
t	a	d	h	e	a

_ _ _ _   _   _ _ _ _ _ _   _ _ _ _ _

_ _ _ _ _ _   _ _ _ _ _   and _ _ _ _

_ _ _ _   on _ _ _ _.   _ _ _ _.

SS885

KING OF THE JEWS

After the soldiers mocked Jesus, they led Him away to crucify Him. Read more about this story by circling every third word beginning with *And*. Write the circled words on the lines found at the bottom of the page. Check your work by reading Matthew 27:35-37.

I came (And) Christ is (they) are you crucified unto his him, in heaven and went Peter parted when Mary his which none garments, the cross casting their nets lots: when spoken that who sees it could Simon might his Father be open Scriptures fulfilled when they which in a was written Pilate spoken Herod is by the Lord the prince of prophet, who came They would look parted garb rock my sheep born garments soldiers did among who could them, a dark and when they upon horses did my cross to vesture cloak hold did when Matthew they thirty pieces cast broke bread lots. About the And did among sitting in doors down red valley they on put watched John and him that sat there; come here And you will set under or up on the over him or his foot and head at you his benefit fact accusation for it written, or drawn THIS or that IS Peter, James, JESUS and with THE queen or KING it is OF my house THE man and JEWS.

Write the verse here.

"And they _____

_____

_____

_____

_____

_____

_____

_____

_____ "

SS885

ON THE CROSS

When Jesus died on the cross, the centurion who stood near Him admitted something very important. To find out what he said, place the letters in the appropriate order according to size and unscramble each word. Place the largest letters on the first blank and unscramble the word. Then place the next to the largest letters on the second blank and unscramble that word. Continue until you have written the complete message. Check your work by reading Mark 15:39.

" _____ _____ _____

_____ _____ _____

_____ _____ ."

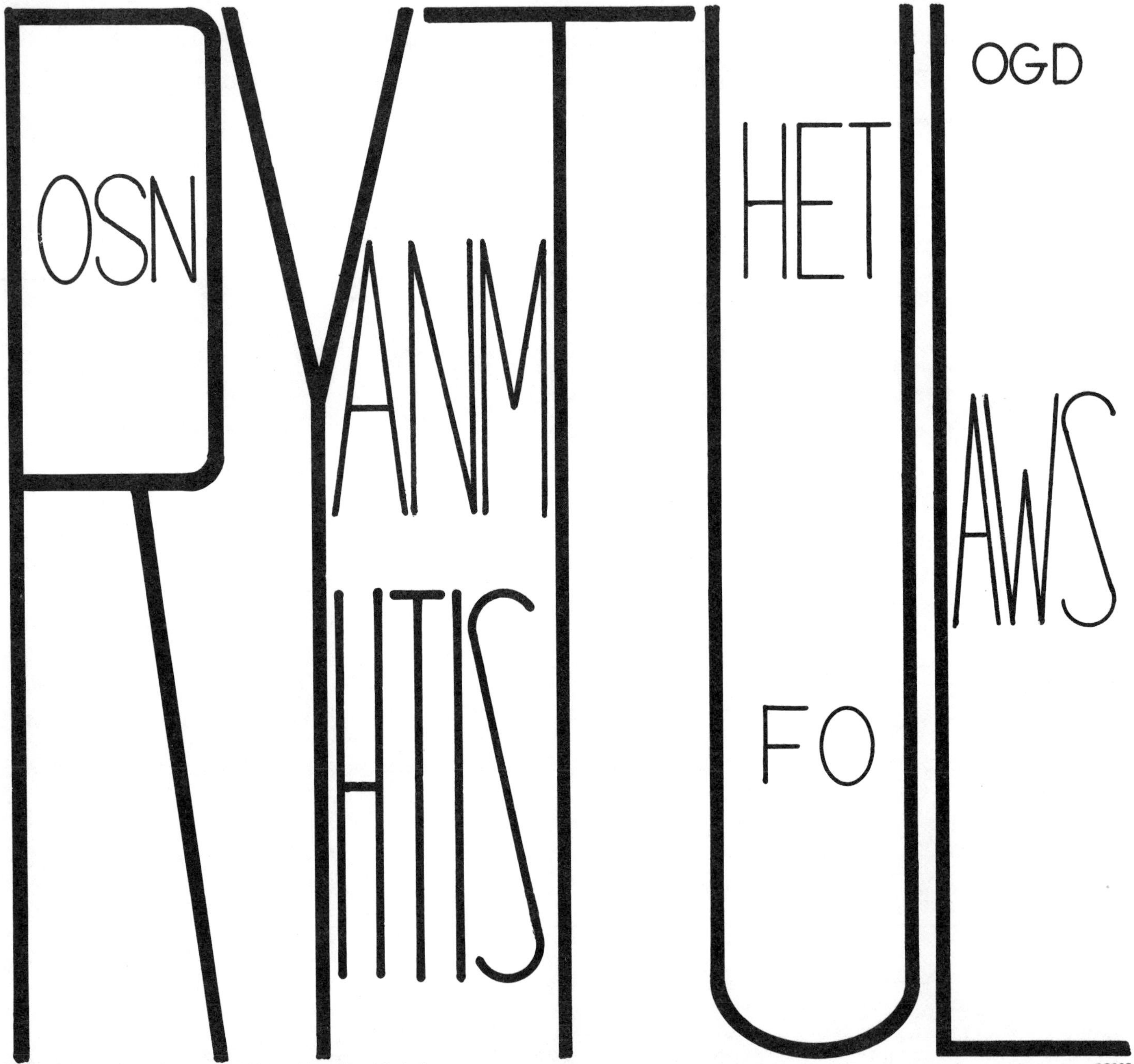

OSN

DVT

RYANM

HET

OGD

R

RHTIS

AWS

FO

UL

SS885

A GREAT EARTHQUAKE

The Resurrection of the Lord is described in Matthew 28:1-3, Mark 16: 1-14; Luke 24:1-49; and John 20:1-23. Can you find a path through the word maze that passes over each word of the Scripture verses in order?

In	In	the	sabbath,	as	it	Magda-lene	back	the	stone	from
the	end	of	the	sabbath,	began	Mary	rolled	stone	door	the
end	of	the	toward	dawn	to	came	and	from	and	sat
of	day	first	day	of	the	week,	came	the	upon	it.
the	sabbath	great	earth-quake:	for	the	angel	and	door,	His	count-enance
week,	came	a	was	white	as	of	heaven,	and	was	like
came	to	see	there	raiment	his	the	from	sat	light-ning	and
Mary	Mary	the	behold,	light-ning	and	Lord	de-scended	upon	his	white
Magda-lene	other	sep-ulchre.	And,	like	was	counte-nance	His	it.	as	snow
and	the	other	Mary	light-ning,	and	his	raiment	white	as	snow:

SS885

THE KEEPERS DID SHAKE

When Jesus was resurrected, there was an earthquake and an angel descended from heaven and rolled back the stone from the door of the tomb. What happened to the guards that witnessed His Resurrection? To discover the answer, you must place the appropriate letter in each square. Squares connected by a line contain the same letter. Check your answer by reading Matthew 28:4.

On another sheet of paper, make a missing letters puzzle like this one, using the Bible verse found in Matthew 28:5.

SS885

ALL HAIL

When the women reached the empty tomb, the angel said to them, "Fear not ye: for I know that ye seek Jesus, which was crucified. He is not here: for he is risen, as he said. Come, see the place where the Lord lay." Then the angel told the woman to go quickly and tell the Disciples that Jesus was in Galilee. To solve this puzzle, write Matthew 28:9 on the lines below. Then fill in the puzzle with every word of the Bible verse. Three words have been filled in for you to get you started.

"

_____

_____

_____

_____ "

PEACE BE UNTO YOU

Jesus had performed many miracles, but His Resurrection was the greatest miracle of all! Place the words from the circles in the squares connected by lines. Squares connected by the same line contain the same word. When you finish the puzzle, check your answer by reading John 20:19.

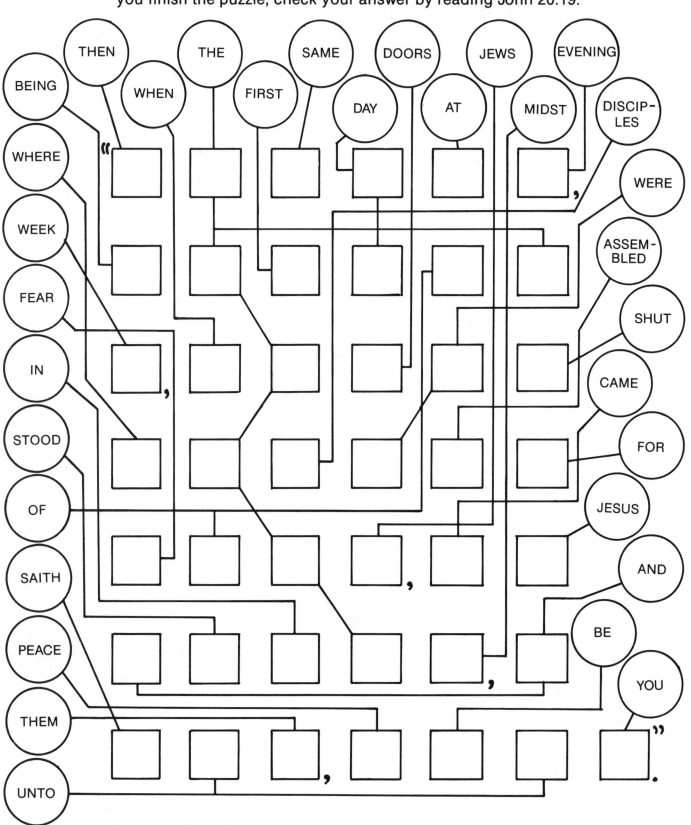

THEY SAW HIM

When Jesus appeared to the Disciples after His Resurrection, they were afraid at first. Use the code found below to find out what the Bible says happened when the Disciples saw Jesus. You must decide what figures represent the vowels. Check your answer by reading Luke 24:37.

B =	C =	D =	F =	G =	H =	J =
K =	L =	M =	N =	P =	Q =	R =
S =	T =	V =	W =	X =	Y =	Z =

A =	E =	I =	O =	U =

WHY ARE YE TROUBLED?

When Jesus appeared to the Disciples, He spoke soft, reassuring words because they were afraid. To discover what Jesus said to the Disciples, unscramble the letters in each word. Write the words on the lines below the scrambled words. Check your work by reading Luke 24:38-40.

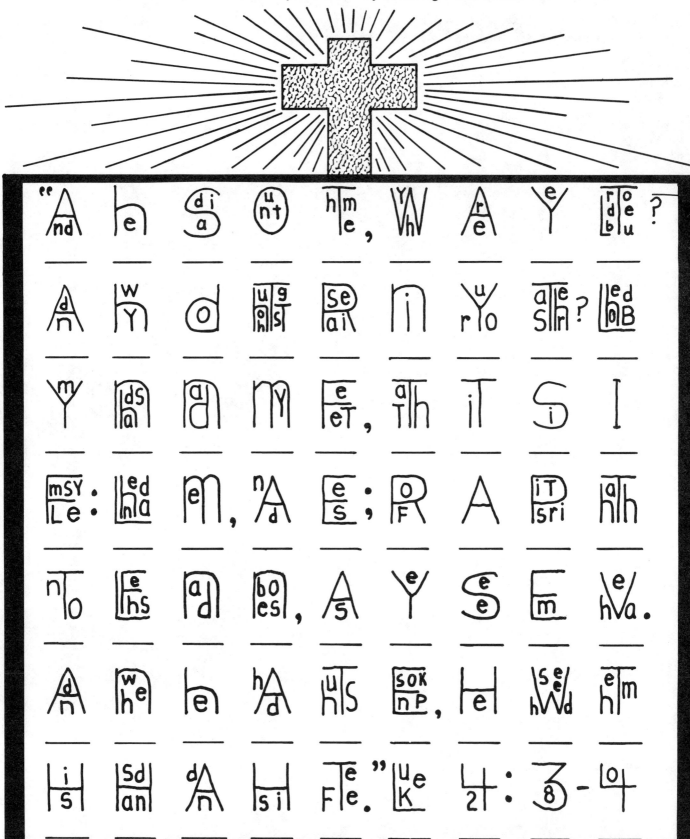

SS885

DOUBTING THOMAS

Thomas, one of the twelve Disciples, was not with the other Disciples when they saw Jesus after His Resurrection. To discover what Thomas said about Jesus' Resurrection, you must change each letter X found below to the appropriate consonant or vowel. All the letters R, S, T, L, N and E have been changed to an X. Check your work by reading John 20:25.

	T e		t e r		
"Xhx	oxhxx		dixcipxxx		xhxxxfoxx
___	_____		_____		_____

xaid	uxxo	him,	Wx	havx
___	___	___	___	___

xxxx	xhx	xoxd.	Bux	hx
___	___	___	___	___

xaid	uxxo	xhxm,	Xxcxpx	I	xhaxx
___	___	___	___	___	___

xxx	ix	hix	haxdx	xhx
___	___	___	___	___

pxixx	of	xhx	xaixx,	axd
___	___	___	___	___

pux	my	fixgxx	ixxo	xhx
___	___	___	___	___

pxixx	of	xhx	xaixx,	axd
___	___	___	___	___

xhxuxx	my	haxd	ixxo	hix
___	___	___	___	___

xidx,	I	wixx	xox	bxxixvx."
___	___	___	___	___

SS885

REACH HITHER

After eight days Jesus came to His Disciples again. This time Thomas was with them. To discover what Jesus said to Thomas, you must change one letter in each word below to form new words. Check your answer by reading John 20:27.

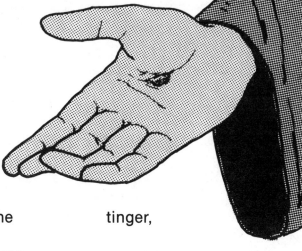

" . . . , Teach   tither   the   tinger,

Reach   _____   ____   _____

end   betold   me   bands;   end

____   _____   ___   _____   ____

peach   huther   the   sand,   ant

_____   _____   ____   _____   ____

thrist   at   unto   me   site:

_____   ____   _____   ___   _____

end   me   got   faithlass,   bat

____   ____   ____   _____   ____

behieving."

_____

Write John 20:28 and change one letter in each word to form new "words." See if a friend can decode your message.

SS885

BLESSED ARE THEY

When Thomas realized that Jesus had truly been resurrected, he said, "My Lord and my God." Then Jesus told Thomas something very important about faith. Read John 20:29 and write it below. Then find a path through the word maze that passes through each letter of the Bible verse in order.

"
_____

_____

_____

_____ "

Jesus	saith	unto	Thomas	yet
saith	him	him,	Thomas,	because	and
saith	seen	hast	thou	and
him	me,	thou	believed:	yet	yet
unto	are	blessed	have	seen,
	they	that	have	not	

MANY SIGNS

To discover the words of the mystery Bible verse, follow each path beginning with path one. Write down the words you pass in the order they are found on the path. Read John 20:30 to check your answer.

Mystery verse: "And   many   _____   _____   _____

_____   _____   _____   _____   _____

_____   _____   _____ ,   _____

_____   _____   _____   _____

_____   _____ ."

1.   2.   3.   4.

book: **written**   **disciples,**   **did**

Make a mystery path puzzle with four paths using the words found in John 20:31. Let a friend solve your puzzle.

YE ARE WITNESSES

Jesus explained to the Disciples that everything that had happened was to fulfill the prophecies of the Old Testament. Then the Disciples understood. To discover what else Jesus told the Disciples, use the word chart found below.

"5h   2d   4d   4h   5a   2g
 And

1i   2a   1a   5a ,   2g   3e

3a   3h ,   1d   1a   3h   4e

4f   4b   1g ,   4b   5c   5i

1a   5e   1b   1a   2e   3f

5g   2b   3b   1f

2h   3c   4c   4g

2i   4a   1c   5b

1e   1a ,   1h   2f

2c .   3f   3d   5d "

5f   3i:3g-4i

	a	b	c	d	e	f	g	h	i
1	And	repentance	beginning	suffer	Jerusalem	preached	dead	Ye	is
2	written	should	witnesses	said	remission	are	it	in	all
3	Christ	be	his	these	behoved	of	46	to	24
4	nations	the	name	unto	rise	from	among	them	48
5	Thus	at	third	things	that	Luke	sins	And	day

SS885

THE PROMISE

Just before Jesus ascended into heaven, He made a promise to His Disciples. To discover the promise, follow the directions carefully. To check your answer, read Luke 24:49.

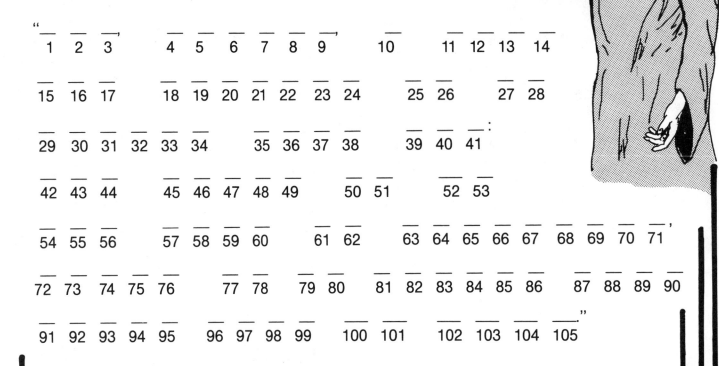

```
"__ __ __,   __ __ __ __ __ __   __   __ __ __ __
  1  2  3     4  5  6  7  8  9    10   11 12 13 14

__ __ __   __ __ __ __ __ __ __   __ __   __ __
15 16 17   18 19 20 21 22 23 24   25 26   27 28

__ __ __ __ __ __   __ __ __ __   __ __ __:
29 30 31 32 33 34   35 36 37 38   39 40 41

__ __ __   __ __ __ __ __   __ __   __ __
42 43 44   45 46 47 48 49   50 51   52 53

__ __ __   __ __ __ __   __ __   __ __ __ __ __ __ __ __ __,
54 55 56   57 58 59 60   61 62   63 64 65 66 67 68 69 70 71

__ __ __ __ __   __ __   __ __   __ __ __ __ __ __   __ __ __ __
72 73 74 75 76   77 78   79 80   81 82 83 84 85 86   87 88 89 90

__ __ __ __ __   __ __ __ __   __ __ __   __ __ __ __ __"
91 92 93 94 95   96 97 98 99  100 101   102 103 104 105
```

Put the letter A in spaces 1, 30, 46 and 68.
Put the letter B in spaces 4, 42 and 79.
Put the letter C in space 57.
Put the letter D in spaces 3, 9, 14, 83 and 86.
Put the letter E in spaces 5, 12, 17, 24, 33, 51, 56, 64, 70, 78, 80, 81, 85 and 94.
Put the letter F in spaces 26, 29, 62 and 96.
Put the letter G in space 104.
Put the letter H in spaces 6, 16, 32, 55, 90, 102 and 105.
Put the letter I in spaces 10, 22, 52, 58, 75, 88 and 103.
Put the letter J in space 63.
Put the letter L in spaces 8, 69 and 76.
Put the letter M in spaces 21, 27, 71 and 99.
Put the letter N in spaces 2, 13, 38, 53, 73, 82 and 101.
Put the letter O in spaces 7, 20, 25, 37, 40, 61, 92, 98 and 100.
Put the letter P in spaces 18, 36 and 91.
Put the letter R in spaces 19, 34, 47, 48, 65, 95 and 97.
Put the letter S in spaces 11, 23 and 67.
Put the letter T in spaces 15, 31, 44, 45, 54, 59, 74 and 89.
Put the letter U in spaces 35, 41, 43, 66, 72 and 84.
Put the letter W in spaces 87 and 93.
Put the letter Y in spaces 28, 39, 49, 50, 60 and 77.

SS885

INTO HEAVEN

Jesus took His Disciples to Bethany. After He lifted up His hands, and blessed them, something miraculous happened. To discover what it was, follow the path and circle every other word you pass in the order the words are found on the path. Then write the words you have circled on the lines found below. Read Luke 24:51 to check your answer.

"And it came _____

_____

_____

_____"

SS885

WHY STAND YE GAZING?

While the Disciples watched Jesus ascending into heaven, two men stood by them in white apparel. To discover what the two men said to the Disciples, you must carefully follow the directions. Check your answer by reading Acts 1:11.

"Wh&ch   #l¢*   ¢#&d,   Y%

Which   also   said   _____

m%n   *f   G#l&l%%,   why

_____   _____   _____   _____

¢!#nd   y%   g#z&ng $p

_____   _____   _____   _____

&n!*   h%#v%n?   !h&¢   ¢#m%

_____   _____   _____   _____

J%¢$¢,   wh&ch   &¢   !#k%n $p

_____   _____   _____   _____   _____

f§*m   y*$ &n!*   h%#v%n,   ¢h#ll

_____   _____   _____   _____   _____

¢*   c*m%   &n   l&k%   m#nn%§   #¢

_____   _____   _____   _____   _____   _____

y%   h#v%   ¢%%n   h&m   g*   &n!*

_____   _____   _____   _____   _____   _____

h%#v%n."

_____

Change all the #'s to the letter A.
Change all the %'s to the letter E.
Change all the &'s to the letter I.
Change all the *'s to the letter O.
Change all the !'s to the letter T.
Change all the ¢'s to the letter S.
Change all the §'s to the letter R.
Change all the $'s to the letter U.

SS885

THEY WENT FORTH

"And they went forth, and preached every where, the Lord working with *them*, and confirming the word with signs following. Amen." Mark 16:20

Since Jesus ascended into heaven, the Disciples and millions of others afterwards have been telling His story. Many symbols are used to represent Jesus. Can you find some of these symbols hidden in the picture? Hidden in the picture are a dove, cross, bread, wine, fish, lamb, crown, lily and Bible.

SS885

ANSWER KEY

Page 5

"From that time forth began Jesus to shew unto his disciples, how that he must go unto Jerusalem, and suffer many things of the elders and chief priests and scribes, and be killed, and be raised again the third day."

Page 6

"Then Peter took him, and began to rebuke him, saying, Be it far from thee, Lord: this shall not be unto thee."

Page 7

"Then said Jesus unto his disciples, If any *man* will come after me, let him deny himself, and take up his cross, and follow me."

Page 8

"Verily I say unto you, There be some standing here, which shall not taste of death, till they see the Son of man coming in his kingdom."

Page 9

"And while they abode in Galilee, Jesus said unto them, The Son of man shall be betrayed into the hands of men:"

Page 10

"And the multitudes that went before, and that followed, cried, saying, Hosanna to the son of David: Blessed *is* he that cometh in the name of the Lord; Hosanna in the highest."

Page 11

"And said unto them, It is written, My house shall be called the house of prayer; but ye have made it a den of thieves."

Page 12

"And the blind and the lame came to him in the temple; and he healed them."

Page 13

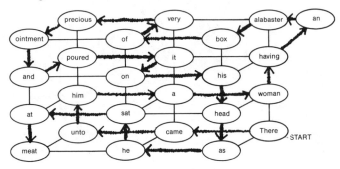

Page 14

"And said *unto them*, What will ye give me, and I will deliver him unto you? And they covenanted with him for thirty pieces of silver. And from that time he sought opportunity to betray him."

Page 15

"And he said, Go into the city to such a man, and say unto him, The Master saith, My time is at hand; I will keep the passover at thy house with my disciples."

Page 16

"Now when the even was come, he sat down with the twelve. And as they did eat, he said, Verily I say unto you, that one of you shall betray me."

Page 17

". . ., That ye love one another; as I have loved you, that ye also love one another."

Page 18

"And as they were eating, Jesus took bread, and blessed *it*, and brake *it*, and gave *it* to the disciples, and said, Take, eat; this is my body.
And he took the cup, and gave thanks, and gave *it* to them, saying, Drink ye all of it;"

Page 19

"Jesus said unto him, Verily I say unto thee, That this night, before the cock crow, thou shalt deny me thrice."

Page 20

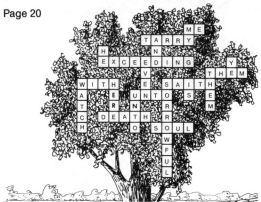

Page 21

"Watch and pray, that ye enter not into temptation: the spirit indeed *is* willing, but the flesh *is* weak. He went away again the second time, and prayed, saying, O my Father, if this cup may not pass away from me, except I drink it, thy will be done."

Page 22

"Then cometh he to his disciples, and saith unto them, Sleep on now, and take *your* rest: behold, the hour is at hand, and the Son of man is betrayed into the hands of sinners."

Page 23

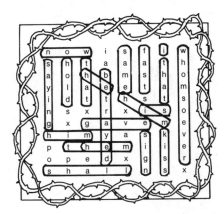

Page 24

"And forthwith he came to Jesus, and said, Hail, master; and kissed him."

Shining Star Publications, Copyright © 1988, A division of Good Apple, Inc.

SS885

Page 25

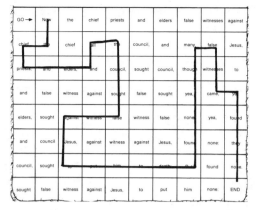

Page 26
"And Peter remembered the word of Jesus, which said unto him, Before the cock crow, thou shalt deny me thrice. And he went out, and wept bitterly."

Page 27
"And he cast down the pieces of silver . . . and hanged himself."

Page 28
They stripped him, and put a scarlet robe on him.
They made a crown of thorns and put it on his head.

Page 29
"And they crucified him, and parted his garments, casting lots: that it might be fulfilled which was spoken by the prophet, They parted my garments among them, and upon my vesture did they cast lots. And sitting down they watched him there; And set up over his head his accusation written, THIS IS JESUS KING OF THE JEWS."

Page 30
". . . , Truly this man was the Son of God."

Page 31

In	In	the	sabbath	as	it	Magda-lene	back	the	stone	from
the	end		the	sabbath,	began	Mary	rolled	stone	door	the
end	of	the	toward	dawn		came	and	from	and	sat
of	day	first	day	of	the	week,	came	the	upon	it.
the	sabbath	great	earth-quake	for	the	angel	and	door	His	count-enance
week,	came	a	was	white	as	of	heaven	and	was	like
came	to	see	there	raiment	his	the	from	sat	light-ning	and
Mary	Mary	the	behold,	light-ning	and	Lord	de-scended	upon	his	white
Magda-lene	other	sep-ulchre.	And,	like	was	counte-nance	His	it.	as	snow
and	the	other	Mary	light-ning,	and	his	raiment	white	as	snow:

Page 32
"And for fear of him the keepers did shake, and became as dead men."

Page 33

Across:
2. they
3. saying
4. and
6. and
8. held
9. feet
10. worshipped
11. as
12. him
16. they
17. behold
18. him
20. met
22. all
23. and

Down:
1. went
2. the
4. and
5. Jesus
7. disciples
8. hail
13. them
14. by
15. tell
18. his
19. came
21. to

Shining Star Publications, Copyright © 1988, A division of Good Apple, Inc.

Page 34
"Then the same day at evening, being the first *day* of the week, when the doors were shut where the disciples were assembled for fear of the Jews, came Jesus and stood in the midst, and saith unto them, Peace *be* unto you."

Page 35
"But they were terrified and affrighted, and supposed that they had seen a spirit."

Page 36
"And he said unto them, Why are ye troubled? and why do thoughts arise in your hearts? Behold my hands and my feet, that it is I myself: handle me, and see; for a spirit hath not flesh and bones, as ye see me have. And when he had thus spoken, he shewed them *his* hands and *his* feet." Luke 24:38-40

Page 37
"The other disciples therefore said unto him, We have seen the Lord. But he said unto them, Except I shall see in his hands the print of the nails, and put my finger into the print of the nails, and thrust my hand into his side, I will not believe."

Page 38
". . . , Reach hither thy finger, and behold my hands; and reach hither thy hand, and thrust *it* into my side: and be not faithless, but believing."

Page 39

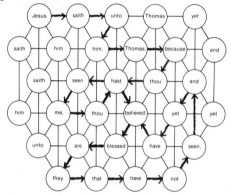

Page 40
"Any many other signs truly did Jesus in the presence of his disciples, which are not written in this book:"

Page 41
"And said unto them, Thus it is written, and thus it behoved Christ to suffer, and to rise from the dead the third day: And that repentance and remission of sins should be preached in his name among all nations, beginning at Jerusalem. And ye are witnesses of these things." Luke 24:46-48

Page 42
"And, behold, I send the promise of my Father upon you: but tarry ye in the city of Jerusalem, until ye be endued with power from on high."

Page 43
"And it came to pass, while he blessed them, he was parted from them, and carried up into heaven."

Page 44
"Which also said, Ye men of Galilee, why stand ye gazing up into heaven? this same Jesus, which is taken up from you into heaven, shall so come in like manner as ye have seen him go into heaven."

Page 45

SS885

CONGRATULATIONS!

FOR COMPLETING ALL THE EASTER PUZZLES

HOSANNA!

Easter Puzzle Award

To: _____

_____
signature

_____
date

Fantastic Work

To: _____

For: _____

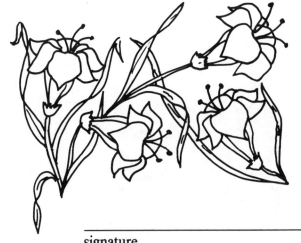

_____
signature

_____
date

SS885

BIBLE EASTER PUZZLES

The puzzles in **BIBLE EASTER PUZZLES** cover the main events from the time Jesus told His disciples of His coming trial, death and resurrection to His ascension into heaven. Brief biblical accounts, followed by codes, mazes and dozens of other highly motivating activities, will make the details of the first Easter come alive for all your Bible students. Each puzzle is Scripture-based, so children can use their Bibles to help them solve the puzzles. Awards and answer key are included.

Books in the Bible Baffler Series

SS881	Bible Crosswords	SS884	Bible Christmas Puzzles
SS882	Bible Word Fun	SS885	Bible Easter Puzzles
SS883	Bible Trivia	SS886	Bible Rebus Puzzles

Meet the Author

Richard Latta lives with his wife, Mary Tripodi Latta, and their four children in Plainfield, Illinois. He is a junior high science teacher. Richard has over forty books in publication and has had material published in **READER'S DIGEST, FAMILY CIRCLE, NATIONAL GEOGRAPHY WORLD** *and many other magazines. His syndicated puzzles have appeared in England, New Zealand, Australia, Sweden, Italy, Malaysia and ten other foreign countries.*

ISBN 0-86653-427-X

Shining Star Publications A Division of Good Apple, Inc.
Box 299, Carthage, IL 62321-0299

495

CALIFORNIA
Here We Come!

BY
PAM MUÑOZ RYAN

ILLUSTRATED BY
KAY SALEM

HOLLYWOOD